Wacky Wheels

by Carol Hosking

Learning Media®

Contents

Introduction

If you want to know who **invented** the wheel, you can go to the library.

If you want to read about cars or trucks, you can click onto the Internet.

But if you want to check out some wheels that are weird, wonderful, or just downright wacky – read this book!

1. All Kinds of Wheels

There are big wheels and tiny wheels.
There are wheels made from wood and
wheels made from metal. All kinds of
wheels make the world go around.

How many kinds of wheels
can you think of?

Here's a store on wheels.
Where will it be the next time
you need to buy something?

Here's a home on wheels. How does the mail find this address?

People use wheels every day. Wheels help us in lots of ways. How have wheels helped you today?

2. Pedal Power

The very first bicycles looked pretty wacky.

One of the first bikes was called a hobbyhorse. It had a seat and a handle for **steering,** but it had no pedals! Riders pushed the bike along with their feet.

It was hard work going uphill ...

but great fun coming down!

One day, a Frenchman called Pierre Michaux had the idea of putting pedals on the hobbyhorse. Pierre called his new **invention** a boneshaker because it was very uncomfortable to ride.

This is another old bike that looks wacky. It's called a penny-farthing. The seat is almost six feet off the ground!

How does the rider get up there?

And, even scarier, how will he get down?

The penny-farthing was named after two British coins – a big penny and a small farthing.

People are always inventing better bikes. They try to make them safer, faster, and more comfortable.

Bicycles have two wheels, which is how the bicycle got its name. "Bi" means "two," and "cycle" means "to go around."

There are other kinds of cycles that have one, three, or four wheels.

Do you think you're good at cycling? Well, try riding this, then. It's a unicycle! (Can you guess what "uni" means?)

A unicycle has one wheel, no **handlebars**, and it has no brakes! The only way to stay on is to keep pedaling.

When you want to stop, you have to pedal slowly and get ready to jump off – fast!

3. Wheels on Your Feet

Why would you want to put wheels on your feet?

There's a story that an ice skater from Holland wanted to ice-skate in summer. But all the ice had melted in spring.

So the skater put two rollers onto wooden boards, then tied the boards onto shoes. This is how roller skates were invented.

Roller skates worked well in a straight line, but they weren't very good for going around corners.

Scott Olson was an ice hockey player from Minnesota. He wanted to practice playing hockey off the ice. Looking at his roller skates, he had an idea. Why not put the wheels in a straight line instead of in pairs?

What a smart idea! He invented in-line skates. In-line skates are fun and fast, and they're great for going around corners!

21

4. Surfing the Sidewalk

How do you **surf** when the waves are too small or when you don't live near the ocean? With a skateboard, you can "surf" the sidewalk.

One day, there were no big waves at a beach in California. The surfers were bored. But, once again, it was wacky wheels to the rescue! The surfers put wheels on the bottom of their surfboards and went surfing on the sidewalk! They invented the skateboard.

Now, people skateboard all over the place. Some people do pretty cool tricks too!

Fact Box

The "ollie" is a skateboard trick – you loop right up into the air on your skateboard.

5. Scoot!

Zip! Zip! You're hip – if you're riding a scooter.

Scooters have a board
like a skateboard, wheels
like in-line skates, and
handlebars like a bike.
Best of all, a scooter's
not too scary. You can
always put one foot
on the ground.

Fact Box

Did you know that scooters aren't a new invention? Scooters were popular when your grandparents were kids. They were made from wood, and they had bigger wheels than scooters do today.

6. Wacky Wheels Parade

Do you want to see some more weird and wacky wheels? Check out our Wacky Wheels Parade!

Ride wacky! Ride safe!

*Calling all wheels – bikes, trikes, wagons ...
to the*

Wacky Wheels Parade

Friday – 10:00 a.m.
Main Street School

*Dress up your wheels in balloons,
flags, streamers ...*

Ride wacky! Ride safe!

We have all kinds of weird and wonderful wheels at our parade.

There are all kinds of wacky people here, too!

You could have your own Wacky Wheels Parade. All you need are a few wheels and some decorations. Then you'll be ready to have a downright wacky day!

Glossary

(These words are printed in bold type the first time they appear in the book.)

handlebar: *a bar to hold onto to steer a bike*

invented: *made something new*

invention: *something that is made for the first time*

steering: *making something go in the right direction*

surf: *to ride on top of a wave on a board*

Index